# of BLESSINGS

Crane Hill Publishers
Birmingham, Alabama

Many thanks to K. Braden Phillips for her help with this book.

Cover illustration by Scott Fuller
Cover design by Alice Pederson

Published by Crane Hill Publishers, 3608 Clairmont Avenue, Birmingham, AL 35222; www.cranehill.com

Printed in the United States of America

Library of Congress Cataloging-in-Publication Data

A pocketful of blessings.
p. cm.
ISBN 1–57587–065–7
1. Benediction. I. Crane Hill Publishers.
BL560.P64 1997
291.4'33–dc21 97–42930
CIP

10 9 8 7 6 5 4 3 2 1

God bless us, every one!

— *Charles Dickens (1812–1870)*

Table of Contents

Blessings for Morning

Father, may I so live the life of love this day that all those with whom I have anything to do may be as sure of love in the world as they are of the sunlight.

— *Author unknown, American prayer*

I reverently speak in the presence of the Great Parent God: I pray that this day, the whole day, as a child of God, I may not be taken hold of by my own desire, but show forth the divine glory by living a life of creativeness, which shows forth the true individual.

— *Traditional Shinto prayer*

O God, as the day returns and brings us the petty round of irritating duties, help us to perform them with laughter and kind faces; let cheerfulness abound with industry. Give us to go blithely on our business all this day, bring us to our resting beds weary and content and undishonored, and grant us in the end the gift of sleep.

— *Robert Louis Stevenson* (1850–1894)

Earth, ourselves,
breathe and awaken,
leaves are stirring,
all things moving,
new day coming,
life renewing.

— *Traditional Pawnee prayer*

And yet, there is only
One great thing,
The only thing:
To live to see in huts and on journeys
The great day that dawns
And the light that fills the world.

— *Traditional Inuit prayer*

O God, Who dividest the day from the night, separate our deeds from the gloom of darkness, that ever meditating on things holy, we may continually live in Thy light; through Jesus Christ our Lord.

— *Traditional Christian prayer*

We give Thee thanks, Lord God of our salvation, because Thou doest all things for the good of our life, that we may always look steadfastly unto Thee, the Savior and Benefactor of our souls; for Thou hast refreshed us in the night past, and raised us up from our beds, and brought us to worship Thy glorious Name. Wherefore we beseech Thee, O Lord, give us grace and power that we may be accounted worthy to sing praise to Thee with understanding, and to pray to Thee without ceasing, in fear and trembling working out our salvation, through the aid of Thy Christ.

— *Traditional Christian prayer*

Our Father, Who art in heaven, hallowed be Thy name. Thy kingdom come. Thy will be done, in earth as it is in heaven. Give us this day our daily bread. And forgive us our trespasses, as we forgive those who trespass against us. And lead us not into temptation, but deliver us from evil. For Thine is the kingdom and the power and the glory forever and ever. Amen.

— *The Lord's Prayer, Traditional*

O Lord, Thou knowest how busy
I must be this day.
If I forget Thee, do not forget me.

— *Jacob Astley (1579–1652)*

Give us grateful hearts, our Father, for all Your mercies, and make us mindful of the needs of others.

— *Traditional Christian prayer*

Give us, O Lord, thankful hearts that never forget Your goodness to us.
Give us, O Lord, grateful hearts that do not waste time complaining.

— *Saint Thomas Aquinas* (1225–1274)

Blessings for EVENING

O Lord, my day's work is over, bless all that I have done aright, and forgive all that has been wrong; and for the remaining hours of this day grant me the peace and rest that come from Thee alone.

— *Traditional Franciscan prayer*

Now I lay me down to sleep, I pray Thee,
Lord, my soul to keep;
If I should die before I wake, I pray Thee,
Lord, my soul to take.

— *Traditional prayer*

Blessed art Thou, Lord our God, King of the universe, who with His word brings on the evenings, with wisdom opens the gates, with understanding alters the phases, varies the seasons, and arranges the stars in their heavenly orbit according to His will. He creates days and night. He rolls away the light from before the darkness and the darkness from before the light, He makes the day to pass and the night to come, and divides between day and night; Lord of hosts is His name. A living and everlasting God, who shall constantly reign over us forever and ever. Blessed art Thou Lord, who brings on the evenings.

— *Traditional Jewish prayer*

Great Father, we are devoutly thankful this evening for material blessings, but we also humbly ask to be fed with the bread of Heaven that we may be strong of mind, pure of heart, fearless of action, and ready to follow wheresoever Thou shalt lead.

— *Traditional Christian prayer*

In the evening and morning and noonday, we praise Thee, we bless Thee, we thank Thee, and we pray Thee, Master of all, to direct our prayer as incense before Thee; and let not our hearts turn away to words or thoughts of wickedness, but rescue us from all things that hunt our souls. For to Thee, Lord, our eyes look up, and our hope is in Thee.

— *Traditional Christian prayer*

O Lord God, the Life of mortals, the Light of the faithful, the Strength of those who labor, and the Repose of the dead; grant us a tranquil night free from all disturbance; that after an interval of quiet sleep, we may, by Thy bounty, at the return of light, be endued with activity from the Holy Spirit, and enabled in security to render thanks to Thee.

— *Traditional Christian prayer*

Blessed art Thou, Almighty Master, Who hast granted us to pass through this day, and to reach the beginning of the night. Hear our prayers, and those of all Thy people; and forgive us our sins voluntary and involuntary, and accept our evening supplications, and send down on Thine inheritance the fullness of Thy mercy and Thy compassion. Compass us about with Thy holy Angels, arm us with the armor of Thy righteousness, fence us round with Thy truth, guard us with Thy power. Deliver us from every assault and every device of the adversary; and grant us to pass this evening and the ensuing night, and all the days of our life, in fullness of peace and holiness, without sin and stumbling. For it is Thine to pity and to save, O Christ our God.

— *Traditional Christian prayer*

O Lord our God, Who didst bow the heavens, and come down for the salvation of mankind, look upon Thy servants and Thine inheritance. For to Thee, the awful and benignant Judge, Thy servants have bowed the head and stooped the neck, looking for no help of man, but waiting for Thy pardon and salvation. Guard them at all times, and this evening, and in the ensuing night, from every foe, from every adverse working of the devil, from idle thoughts, and wicked imaginations.

— *Traditional Christian prayer*

Keep watch, Dear Lord, with those who work, or watch, or weep this night, and give Your angels charge over those who sleep. Tend the sick, Lord Christ; give rest to the weary, bless the dying, soothe the suffering, pity the afflicted, shield the joyous; and all for Your love's sake.

— *Saint Augustine* (354–430)

I see the moon, and the moon sees me.
God bless the moon, and God bless me.

— *Author unknown*

From ghoulies and ghosties and long
leggety beasties
And things that go bump in the night,
Good Lord, deliver us.

— *Traditional Scottish prayer*

Blessings for MEALTIMES

O God, who makes a thousand flowers
to blow,
Who makes both grains and fruits to grow,
Hear our prayer:
Bless this food
And bring us peace.

— *Author unknown*

Lord, behold our family here assembled.
We thank You for this place in which
we dwell,
for the love that unites us,
for the peace accorded us this day,
for the hope with which we expect the
morrow;
for the health, the work, the food, and
the bright skies that make our
lives delightful;
for our friends in all parts of the earth.

— *Robert Louis Stevenson (1850–1894)*

O You who feed the little bird,
bless our food, O Lord.

— *Traditional Norwegian prayer*

O God, you fill the hungry with good things. Send your blessing on us, as we work in the kitchen, and make us ever thankful for our daily bread. Grant this through Christ our Lord.

— *Traditional Basque prayer*

Thank you for the wind and the rain
and sun and pleasant weather,
thank you for this our food and that
we are together.

— *Traditional Mennonite prayer*

El Shaddai,
You are the earth beneath our feet,
the ground of our being,
and the Womb of all.
You birth the earth,
groaning with great labor pain
  in all our suffering and dying.
Your golden joys and scarlet sorrows
fall onto death's dark soil,
and nourish the grain that becomes
  the Bread of Life.
We harvest Your bounty,
we feast on Your beauty,
and are nourished and comforted
  at the breasts of Your goodness.

— *Author unknown*

Round the table
Peace and joy prevail.
May all who share
this season's delight
enjoy countless more.

— *Traditional Chinese prayer*

Some ha'e meat and can-na eat,
And some ha'e none that want it;
But we ha'e meat and we can eat,
And so the Lord be thank-et.

— *Robert Burns* (1759–1796)

Us and this, God bless.

— *Traditional Quaker prayer*

God is great and God is good
And we thank Him for our food.
By His hand we all are fed;
Give us, Lord, our daily bread.

— *Traditional prayer*

Heavenly Father, bless us,
  and keep us all alive.
There's ten of us to dinner
  and not enough for five.

— *Author unknown*

Blessings for Special Occasions

Wedding

Almighty God, Who at the beginning did create our first parents, Adam and Eve, and did sanctify and join them together in marriage; Pour upon you the riches of His grace, sanctify and bless you, that ye may please Him both in body and soul, and live together in holy love unto your lives' end.

— *Traditional Christian prayer*

Wedding

May the Great Spirit send his choicest
gifts to you,
May the Sun father and Moon mother shed
their softest beams on you,
May the four winds of heaven blow gently
upon you and upon those with whom
you share your heart and home.

— *Traditional Coahuila prayer*

Wedding

May the bridesmaids
all night long
sing of the love
of you and your bride,
adorned with violets.

— *Sappho* (c. 610–c. 580 B.C.)

Wedding

I add my breath to your breath that our days may be long on the Earth, that the days of our people may be long, that we shall be as one person, that we may finish our road together.

— *Traditional Laguna Pueblo prayer*

Birth of a Child

That she was taken out of her mother,
thanks be for that!
That she, the little one, was taken
out of her, we say, thanks be for that!

— *Traditional Inuit prayer*

Birth or Adoption of a Child

Our Father, we ask Thee to bless us. We thank Thee for the new life that has come into our home. We bring it to Thee in consecration. We would lay it in Thine arms. We would ask for Thy divine keeping of it. We cannot keep it, for the world is very full of evil. Thou alone canst guard it from harm. We ask Thee for grace to make our home a fit place for this precious life to grow up in. Help us to make it a place of love, a place of prayer, a place of all beautiful living, a place sweet with heaven's fragrance. Make us fit to hold this child in our arms, to clasp it to our bosom, to be its teachers and guides. Help us to answer its questions, to solve its problems, and be to it a pattern of holy living.

— *Traditional Christian prayer*

Birth or Adoption of a Child

My sun!

My morning star!

Help this child to become a man.

I name him

Rain-dew Falling!

I name him

Star Mountain!

— *Traditional Tewa prayer*

Competition

Good Lord, help me to win if I may,
and if I may not, help me to be
a good loser.

— *Author unknown*

Blessings for HOME

May the roof of your house never fall in,
And those under it never fall out.

— *Traditional Irish prayer*

Dwell in this home; never be parted!
Enjoy the full duration of your days,
with sons and grandsons playing to the end,
rejoicing in your home to your heart's
content.

— *Traditional Hindu prayer*

God, let our home be friendly,
With open doors to all
Who come for food and shelter
Or just to pay a call.
And give us grace in sharing
Our best with every guest
That each may feel the comfort
Of warmth Thy love has blest.

— *Author unknown*

O my guardians, from remote antiquity, watch over our home from top to bottom; from one corner to the other; from east to west; from the side facing the sea; from the inside to the outside, watch over and protect it; ward off all that may trouble our life here.

— *Traditional Hawaiian prayer*

Almighty and everlasting God, be Thou present to our duties, and grant the protection of Thy presence to all that dwell in this house; that Thou mayest be known to be the Defender of Thy family, and the Inhabitant of this dwelling; through Jesus Christ our Lord.

— *Traditional Christian prayer*

Blessings for PEACE

The Lord bless us and keep us,
the Lord make His face to shine upon us,
and be gracious unto us, the Lord lift up
the light of His countenance upon us and
give us peace.

— *Traditional Christian prayer*

The peace of God, which passeth all understanding, keep your hearts and minds in the knowledge and love of God, and of His son Jesus Christ our Lord: and the blessing of God Almighty, the Father, the Son, and the Holy Ghost, be amongst you and remain with you always.

— *Traditional Christian prayer*

O God, give us peace, give us tranquillity, and let good fortune come to us. Let the one who put a jinx on the village die. Let him die, he who thought evil thoughts against us. Also give us fish.

— *Traditional Wapokomo prayer*

Let peace abound in our small company. Purge out of every heart the lurking grudge. Give us grace and strength to forbear and to persevere. Offenders ourselves, give us the grace to accept and to forgive offenders. Forgetful, help us to bear cheerfully the forgetfulness of others. Give us courage and gaiety and the quiet mind.

— *Traditional Christian prayer*

Deep peace of the running wave to you,
Deep peace of the flowing air to you,
Deep peace of the quiet earth to you,
Deep peace of the shining stars to you,
Deep peace of the gentle night to you,
Moon and stars pour their healing light
on you.
Deep peace to you.

— *Traditional Gaelic prayer*

Creator of the world
Help us love one another,
Help us care for each other
As sister or brother,
That friendship may grow
From nation to nation
Bring peace to our world
O Lord of Creation.

— *Author unknown*

Lord God Almighty, Christ the King of glory, Who art our true Peace, and Love eternal; enlighten our souls with the brightness of Thy peace, and purify our consciences with the sweetness of Thy love, that we may with peaceful hearts wait for the Author of peace, and in the adversities of this world may ever have Thee for our Guardian and Protector; and so being fenced about by Thy care, may heartily give ourselves to the love of Thy peace.

— *Traditional Christian prayer*

O God, Who are Peace everlasting, Whose chosen reward is the gift of peace, and Who hast taught us that the peacemakers are Thy children, pour Thy sweet peace into our souls, that everything discordant may utterly vanish, and all that makes for peace be sweet to us for ever.

— *Traditional Christian prayer*

O Creator, Thou who sayest, "Let there be night," the dawn, the day, the sunset, Grant to the Sun, Your son, that when he rises, he may give light to the men whom Thou hast created.
O Creator, O Sun, who art in peace and well-being, give light to this nation, keep it ever sane and happy.

— *Traditional Peruvian prayer*

Forgive me, Lord, for Thy dear Son,
The ill that I this day have done,
That with the world, myself, and Thee,
I, ere I sleep, at peace may be.

— *Thomas Ken (1637–1711)*

Lord, help me to find the good and praise it.

— *Author unknown*

Fill Your children with kindness, wisdom, and love. Then shall they learn to live at peace. Blessed is the Lord, Teacher of Peace.

— *Traditional Jewish prayer*

Have mercy on me, O Beneficent One. I was angered for I had no shoes; then I met a man who had no feet.

— *Traditional Chinese prayer*

Lord, make me an instrument of Thy peace; where there is hatred, let me sow love; where there is injury, pardon; where there is discord, union; where there is doubt, faith; where there is despair, hope; where there is darkness, light; where there is sadness, joy.

O Divine Master, grant that I may not so much seek to be consoled as to console; to be understood as to understand; to be loved as to love. For it is in giving that we receive, it is in pardoning that we are pardoned, and it is in dying that we are born to eternal life.

— *Saint Francis of Assisi (1182–1226)*

Blessings for Well-Being and Safety

May the road rise to meet you.
May the wind be always at your back.
May the sun shine warm upon your face.
May the rains fall softly upon your fields
  until we meet again.
May God hold you in the hollow
  of his hand.

— *Traditional Gaelic prayer*

Let the earth of my body be mixed
with the earth my beloved walks on.
Let the fire of my body be the brightness
in the mirror that reflects his face.
Let the water of my body join the waters
of the lotus pool he bathes in.
Let the breath of my body be air lapping
his tired limbs.
Let me be sky, and moving through me
that cloud-dark Shyama, my beloved.

— *Traditional Hindu prayer*

O God, scatterer of ignorance
  and darkness, grant me your strength.
May all beings regard me with the eye
  of a friend, and I all beings!
With eye of a friend may each single being
  regard all others!

— *Traditional Hindu prayer*

God bless all those that I love;
God bless all those that love me;
God bless all those that love those
that I love
And all those that love those that love me.

— *Author unknown*

Weave for us a garment of brightness; may the warp be the white light of morning, may the weft be the red light of evening, may the fringes be the falling rain, may the border be the standing rainbow. Thus weave for us a garment of brightness, that we may walk fittingly where birds sing, that we may walk fittingly where grass is green, O our Mother the Earth, O our Father the Sky.

— *Traditional Native American prayer*

Almighty God, our heavenly Father, who of his great mercy hath promised forgiveness of sins to all them that with hearty repentance and true faith turn unto him; Have mercy upon you; pardon and deliver you from all your sins; confirm and strengthen you in all goodness; and bring you to everlasting life; through Jesus Christ our Lord.

— *Traditional Christian prayer*

God be in my head, and in my
understanding;
God be in my eyes, and in my looking;
God be in my mouth, and in my speaking;
God be in my heart, and in my thinking;
God be at my end, and in my departing.

— *Traditional English prayer*

Naked you came
  from Earth the Mother
Naked you return to her.
May a good wind be your road.

— *Traditional Omaha prayer*

Bless our children with healthful bodies, with good understandings, with the graces and gifts of Thy Spirit, with sweet dispositions and holy habits; and sanctify them throughout in their bodies, souls, and spirits; and keep them blameless until the coming of our Lord Jesus.

— *Jeremy Taylor (1613–1667)*

Our eyes may see some uncleanness,
but let not our mind see things
that are not clean.
Our ears may hear some uncleanness,
but let not our mind hear things
that are not clean.

— *Traditional Shinto prayer*

Protect me, O Lord, for my boat is so small and Your sea is so big.

— *Traditional Breton fishermen's prayer*

Thou Who hast given so much to me,
Give one thing more, a grateful heart.
Not thankful when it pleaseth me,
As if blessings had spare days,
But such a heart, whose pulse may
be praise.

— *George Herbert (1593–1633)*

May the passions of lust, anger, greed, pride, and attachment depart from me. O Lord, I come to seek shelter; Bless me with grace.

— *Traditional Sikh prayer*

May there always be work for your hands
to do,
May your purse always hold a coin or two,
May the sun always shine upon your
windowpane,
May a rainbow be certain to follow
each rain,
May the hand of a friend always be near
to you, and
May God fill your heart with gladness
to cheer you.

— *Traditional Irish prayer*

Incline us, O God, to think humbly of ourselves, to be saved only in the examination of our own conduct, to consider our fellow creatures with kindness, and to judge of all they say and do with the charity which we would desire from them ourselves.

— *Jane Austen* (1775–1817)

In soft whisperings from the heart,
The child within offers you always
The thread of your truth.
May you cherish that child, trust
That voice and weave that thread
Richly into the fabric of your days.

— Author unknown

May those who love us, love us
And those who don't love us,
May God turn their hearts,
And if He doesn't turn their hearts,
May He turn their ankles
So we'll know them by their limping.

— *Traditional Gaelic prayer*

May the strength of God pilot me, the power of God preserve me today. May the wisdom of God instruct me, the eye of God watch over me, the ear of God hear me, the word of God give me sweet talk, the hand of God defend me, and the way of God guide me.

— *Saint Patrick (fifth century)*

Give us, O Lord, thankful hearts which never forget Your goodness to us.
Give us, O Lord, grateful hearts, which do not waste time complaining.

— *Saint Thomas Aquinas* (1225–1274)

Every passing year makes my life shorter, and time that is gone can never be recalled. Assist me, Ahura Mazda, to be wise from the experiences of the past and to move into the future with love and hope. Guide me to make the best use of each day and each opportunity as they come so that I may glorify the name of my ancestors, my religion, my community, and my country. Grant me clear and pure mind, I pray, and devotion to Thee in everything I say or do. May the heavenly sun light my way for many a year to come and may love and blessings always be with me in life. May I always remain worthy of love!

— *Traditional Zoroastrian prayer*

Dear Father, hear and bless beasts
and singing birds;
And guard with tenderness small things
that have no words.

— *Author unknown*

Lord, purge our eyes to see
Within the seed a tree,
Within the glowing egg a bird,
Within the shroud a butterfly.
Till taught by such, we see
Beyond all creatures Thee,
And hearken to tender word,
And hear it, "Fear not: It is I."

— *Christina Rossetti* (1830–1894)

O God, make speed to save us,
O Lord, make haste to help us.

— *Traditional Christian prayer*

Keep us, O Lord, as the apple of Your eye;
Hide us under the shadow of Your wings.

— *Traditional Christian prayer*

From silly devotions and from sour-faced saints, Good Lord, deliver us.

— *Saint Teresa of Avila* (1515–1582)